Catherine, The Future Queen of Wales

A Biography of Grace, Secrets, and Strength

Harriet Montgomery

Preface

A Journey of Grace, Secrets, and Strength

"I really hope I can make a difference, even in the smallest way. I am looking forward to helping as much as I can." These words, spoken by Catherine, Princess of Wales, during her first post-engagement interview in 2010, encapsulate the essence of her life and her approach to her role within the British royal family.

This biography, "Catherine: The Future Queen of Wales - A Biography of Grace, Secrets, and Strength," looks into the remarkable journey of a woman who has not only captured the heart of Prince William but also the hearts of millions around the world.

Catherine's story is one of ordinary beginnings leading to extraordinary outcomes. Born on January 9, 1982, in Reading, Berkshire, she grew up in the picturesque village of Bucklebury, where her family's modest home and close-knit community instilled in her the values of hard work, family unity, and compassion. Her upbringing, marked by a supportive family and a strong educational foundation, laid the groundwork for her future as a member of the royal family.

This biography explores Catherine's formative years, her education at St. Andrew's School and Marlborough College, and her time at the University of St. Andrews, where she met Prince William. It digs into the romance and challenges of their engagement, the grandeur of their wedding, and the significant milestones of her life as a royal, including her charitable work, her role as a mother, and her recent health crisis.

Throughout this narrative, we uncover the secrets and traditions of the royal family, highlighting Catherine's unique approach to her duties and her commitment to making a positive impact. Her journey is a testament to her strength and resilience, qualities that have been evident from her early days as a young woman navigating the complexities of royal life.

As we follow Catherine's path, we are reminded of her aspirations to make a difference, no matter how small. Her dedication to causes such as early childhood care, addiction, and mental health awareness reflects her genuine desire to serve and inspire. This book is not just a biography; it is a celebration of a woman who embodies the very essence of grace, secrets, and strength.

In the following pages, we invite you to join us on this journey through Catherine's life, a journey that is as inspiring as it is informative. Her story is a powerful reminder that even the smallest actions can have a profound impact and that with determination, compassion, and strength, one can overcome any challenge and achieve greatness.

Table of Content

Introduction

Few figures in British royal history have captured the public's imagination quite like Catherine, Princess of Wales. Her story - from a middle-class upbringing to the brink of queenship - bridges centuries of tradition with the demands of a modern monarchy. As we explore Catherine's life, we witness the making of a 21st-century royal icon, a woman whose influence will shape one of the world's oldest institutions.

Catherine Elizabeth Middleton was born on January 9, 1982, in Reading, England, far from palaces and royal expectations. The eldest child of Michael and Carole Middleton, Catherine's early years were comfortable but decidedly non-aristocratic. Her parents, former British Airways employees who built a successful party supplies business, gave Catherine and her siblings a stable, loving home. This foundation would prove crucial in navigating the challenges of royal life.

Catherine's life changed forever at the University of St Andrews in Scotland. In 2001, she met Prince William, heir to the British throne. Their friendship blossomed into romance, captivating a nation and soon, the world. Their courtship - from university sweethearts to a brief separation and eventual reunion - read like a modern fairy tale, but with added pressures of intense media scrutiny and royal expectations.

Their 2010 engagement marked Catherine's official entry into royal life. The sapphire and diamond ring on her finger - once worn by William's mother, the late Princess Diana - symbolized not just a promise of marriage, but a passing of the torch. Catherine was stepping into a role demanding grace under pressure, strength in adversity, and the ability to keep parts of her life private.

Millions around the globe watched the royal wedding on April 29, 2011. Catherine, resplendent in her Alexander McQueen gown, walked down Westminster Abbey's aisle not just as a bride, but as a future queen. The world held its breath, wondering: How would this young woman, with no royal blood, adapt to the demands of her new role?

In the years that followed, Catherine answered that question with remarkable poise and dedication. She immersed herself in royal duties, carefully selecting charitable causes close to her heart. Early childhood development became a cornerstone of her work, with Catherine emphasizing the crucial importance of a child's first five years. Her "Five Big Questions" survey on early childhood development in 2020 showed her commitment to evidence-based approaches in tackling societal issues.

Mental health awareness is another cause Catherine champions. Alongside Prince

William and Prince Harry, she spearheaded the "Heads Together" campaign, working to destigmatize mental health issues and promote open conversations about emotional wellbeing. This initiative not only raised awareness but also showcased Catherine's ability to connect with people from all walks of life, from schoolchildren to veterans.

As she grew into her role, Catherine's influence on the monarchy became increasingly apparent. Her approachable demeanor and relatable interests - from photography to gardening - helped bridge the gap between the royals and the public. She brought a fresh, modern sensibility to ancient traditions, all while respecting the institution's history and protocol.

But life as a royal is never without its challenges. Catherine faced intense media scrutiny from the moment her relationship with William became public. Every outfit, every public appearance, and every perceived misstep became fodder for tabloid headlines. The pressure to be perfect, to always present a flawless image to the world, is a burden few can truly understand.

It's in how Catherine has handled these pressures that we see her true strength emerge. Whether facing criticism over her fashion choices or navigating family tensions played out on a global stage, she has maintained a dignified silence, letting her actions speak louder than any rebuttal could.

This strength was put to the ultimate test in early 2024 when Catherine faced a personal health crisis that shocked the nation. The announcement of her cancer diagnosis and subsequent treatment thrust her into an entirely new spotlight. Suddenly, the woman known for her composure and grace was fighting a battle that millions could relate to on a deeply personal level.

Catherine's handling of this challenge speaks volumes about her character. Her decision to be open about her diagnosis, to share her journey with the public, has been met with an outpouring of support. It has also humanized the royal family in a way few events could, reminding the world that behind the titles and tiaras are real people facing real struggles.

Throughout this ordeal, Prince William's unwavering support has been evident. Their partnership, tested by the fires of public life and personal trials, stands as a testament to the strength of their bond. Together, they present a united front - not just as royals, but as parents, partners, and public servants.

Speaking of parenthood, Catherine's role as a mother to Prince George, Princess Charlotte, and Prince Louis adds another layer to her public persona. She has been vocal about the joys and challenges of raising children in the public eye, striving to give them as normal an upbringing as possible within the confines of royal life. Her hands-on approach to parenting, from school runs to family outings, has endeared her to many who see in her a relatable figure despite her extraordinary circumstances.

As we dig deeper into Catherine's story, we'll explore the many facets of her life and role. We'll examine how she balances tradition with modernity, duty with personal fulfillment, and public expectations with private realities. We'll look at the causes she champions, the people she's touched, and the legacy she's building.

But beyond the public figure, this biography seeks to understand Catherine the person. What drives her? What are her hopes and fears? How does she navigate the complex web of relationships within the royal family? And what secrets lie behind the carefully managed public image?

The themes of grace, secrets, and strength run throughout Catherine's story. Her grace is evident in every public appearance, in the way she carries herself with dignity and warmth whether meeting world leaders or comforting a child. It's in the thoughtful way she approaches her role, never overshadowing but always supporting, embodying the ideal of a modern princess.

The secrets aspect of Catherine's life is perhaps the most intriguing. Life within palace walls has always been mysterious, and Catherine now holds the keys to some of the monarchy's most closely guarded traditions and protocols. What really goes on during state banquets? How are royal children educated in the ways of court life? And how does one prepare to someday wear the crown? These are just some of the questions we'll seek to answer.

But it's Catherine's strength that truly defines her journey. From withstanding the pressures of public scrutiny to facing personal health challenges, she has shown a resilience that goes beyond mere stoicism. It's a strength born of purpose, of understanding the importance of her role not just to the monarchy, but to the millions who look to her as a role model and source of inspiration.

As we embark on this exploration of Catherine's life, we do so knowing we're witnessing history unfold. The choices she makes, the causes she champions, and the way she adapts the role of Princess of Wales for a new era will have repercussions for generations to come.

This biography aims to paint a comprehensive picture of Catherine - the girl from Berkshire who captured a prince's heart, the young woman who stepped onto the world stage with poise and purpose, and the future queen who is redefining what it means to be royal in the 21st century.

Through interviews with those who know her, analysis of her public work, and careful examination of her impact on the monarchy and British society, we'll attempt to understand the real Catherine. We'll celebrate her triumphs, acknowledge her struggles, and speculate on the mark she'll leave on history.

As Catherine continues to write her own chapter in the long story of the British monarchy, one thing is clear: she is a figure of profound significance, not just for her future role as queen, but for what she represents - a bridge between the ancient and the modern, tradition and progress, duty and compassion.

In the pages that follow, we'll unravel the complexities of Catherine's world. We'll explore the grace that defines her public persona, uncover the secrets that add intrigue to her story, and celebrate the strength that has carried her through both triumph and adversity.

This is the story of Catherine, Princess of Wales - a tale of transformation, of duty, and destiny, and of a woman who continues to captivate and inspire. As we turn the page on this introduction and dive into the chapters of her life, we invite you to discover the many layers of a truly remarkable royal figure - one who is shaping the future of the monarchy with every step she takes.

Catherine Elizabeth Middleton: The Early Years

"I think I know I can't really change my nature, but I've learned to sort of adapt." - Catherine, Princess of Wales

Born on a crisp winter's day, January 9, 1982, in Reading, Berkshire, Catherine Elizabeth Middleton entered the world with little fanfare. No one could have predicted that this newborn girl would one day become the Princess of Wales and future Queen Consort of the United Kingdom. Her story began not in a palace, but in the cozy confines of the Royal Berkshire Hospital, marking the start of a journey that would captivate millions around the globe.

The Middleton Family: A Foundation of Love and Entrepreneurship

Catherine's parents, Michael and Carole Middleton, met while working as flight attendants for British Airways. Their romance blossomed amidst the clouds, and they married in 1980, settling into a modest home in Bradfield Southend. Michael, born to a middle-class family in Leeds, and Carole, whose ancestors were coal miners and builders from Durham, embodied the essence of hard work and ambition.

In 1987, the Middletons' entrepreneurial spirit led them to establish Party Pieces, a mail-order business selling party supplies and decorations. What began as a small venture run from their home soon burgeoned into a multimillion-pound enterprise. This success allowed the family to move to the picturesque village of Bucklebury in Berkshire, providing

Catherine and her siblings with a childhood steeped in the idyllic English countryside.

Catherine's early years were marked by the close-knit bonds of family life. As the eldest of three children, she often took on a protective role towards her younger siblings, Philippa (Pippa) and James. The Middleton household was one of warmth, encouragement, and stability – qualities that would later shape Catherine's approach to her own family life and royal duties.

A Childhood of Privilege and Normalcy

While the Middletons' business success afforded their children certain privileges, Catherine's upbringing remained remarkably grounded. Her parents instilled in her the values of hard work, humility, and the importance of education. Weekends were often spent exploring the rolling hills of Berkshire, picnicking in meadows, or helping out in the family business – experiences that fostered Catherine's love for the outdoors and her down-to-earth nature.

Catherine's early education began at St. Andrew's School in Pangbourne, where she quickly distinguished herself as both an academic and athletic standout. It was here that the foundations of her future grace and poise began to take shape. Teachers remember her as a diligent student with a keen interest in the arts and literature, foreshadowing her later patronage of cultural institutions.

An amusing anecdote from her St. Andrew's days reveals Catherine's early brush with *'royalty'*. During a school production of *"Cinderella,"* she was cast as the lead, opposite a young boy playing Prince Charming. Little did anyone know that this role was a prescient glimpse into her future.

Marlborough College: Shaping a Future Princess

At 13, Catherine enrolled at the prestigious Marlborough College in Wiltshire. This co-educational boarding school, known for its rigorous academic standards and diverse extracurricular offerings, provided the perfect environment for Catherine to flourish. Here, her innate qualities of leadership, resilience, and grace began to truly shine.

Catherine's time at Marlborough was marked by a series of accomplishments that hint at the remarkable woman she would become. She excelled academically, particularly in art and English literature, subjects that continue to influence her public work today. But it was on the sports field where Catherine truly came into her own.

As captain of the school's field hockey team, Catherine demonstrated not just athletic prowess but also leadership skills that would serve her well in her future role. Her teammates recall her as a fierce competitor with an uncanny ability to motivate and unite the team. This experience in leadership and teamwork undoubtedly contributed to her later ease in public roles and her ability to connect with people from all walks of life.

Lesser-known to many, Catherine also set a school record in the high jump, clearing 1.50 meters. This physical feat is emblematic of her ability to rise above challenges – a trait that would prove invaluable in her later life in the public eye.

Despite her achievements, Catherine's time at Marlborough wasn't without its challenges. In her early teens, she faced bullying from some classmates. However, rather than allowing this to defeat her,

Catherine used these experiences to develop resilience and empathy – qualities that have become hallmarks of her public persona and her work with mental health initiatives.

A Gap Year of Growth and Discovery

Following her graduation from Marlborough in 2000, Catherine made the decision to take a gap year – a choice that would prove transformative. This year of exploration and self-discovery took her from the historic streets of Florence to the rugged landscapes of Chile, broadening her horizons and shaping her worldview.

In Florence, Catherine immersed herself in the study of Italian language and Renaissance art at the British Institute. This experience not only honed her linguistic skills but also deepened her appreciation for art and culture. Her time in Italy would later influence her choices as a patron of the arts and her approach to cultural diplomacy.

Perhaps the most formative experience of her gap year was Catherine's participation in the Raleigh International programme in Chile. For ten weeks, she engaged in community projects and wilderness expeditions in Patagonia. This challenging environment tested her physical and mental endurance, fostering a sense of independence and adaptability.

During her time in Chile, Catherine worked on environmental projects, helped build facilities for rural communities, and even embarked on scuba diving expeditions. These experiences cultivated her interest in environmental conservation and community development – themes that would later become central to her royal work.

A little-known fact from this period reveals Catherine's adventurous spirit. During a particularly grueling hike in the Andes, she volunteered to lead her group through a treacherous pass, displaying a level of courage and leadership that impressed both her peers and instructors.

The Road to St. Andrews

As Catherine's gap year drew to a close, she set her sights on the University of St. Andrews in Scotland. Her choice of university would prove fateful, not just for her academic pursuits but for her personal life as well.

Initially, Catherine had secured a place at the University of Edinburgh. However, in a decision that would alter the course of her life, she chose to take a year out and reapply to St. Andrews. This choice was influenced by her desire to study art history, but it also aligned with the plans of another notable student – Prince William.

While speculation has long swirled about whether Catherine deliberately chose St.

Andrews to meet the prince, those close to her insist it was a genuine academic decision. Regardless of the motivation, this choice set the stage for one of the most famous love stories of the modern era.

As Catherine prepared for university, she spent several months working as a deckhand on round-the-world challenge boats in Southampton. This experience further developed her love for sailing and the sea – interests she would later share with Prince William and incorporate into her royal duties.

The Foundations of a Future Queen

Catherine's early life laid the groundwork for the woman she would become – a future Queen known for her grace, resilience, and commitment to public service. Her childhood in Bucklebury instilled in her a love for the simple pleasures of country life and a strong sense of family values. Her education at St. Andrew's School and Marlborough College honed her academic abilities and leadership skills, while her gap year experiences broadened her worldview and fostered her independence.

Throughout these formative years, Catherine demonstrated a remarkable ability to adapt to new situations and rise to challenges – qualities that would serve her well in her future role as a member of the royal family. Her early life was characterized by a balance of privilege and normalcy, academic achievement and athletic prowess, and a growing sense of social responsibility.

As Catherine stood on the cusp of adulthood, preparing to embark on her university career at St. Andrews, she carried with her the values, experiences, and qualities that would shape her into the Princess of Wales we know today. Her journey from a middle-class girl in Berkshire to a beacon of modern royalty was just beginning, but the foundations were already firmly in place.

The story of Catherine's early years is not just a tale of a future princess, but a narrative of personal growth, resilience, and the power of a supportive family environment. It's a testament to the idea that while destiny may play a role, it's our experiences, choices, and responses to challenges that truly shape who we become.

As we move deeper into Catherine's life in the subsequent chapters, we'll see how these early experiences influenced her approach to royal duties, her charitable work, and her role as a wife and mother. The grace, secrets, and strength that define Catherine, the Future Queen of Wales, all have their roots in these formative years – a childhood and youth that prepared her, perhaps unknowingly, for the extraordinary life that lay ahead.

The Royal Engagement: A Tale of Love, Destiny, and National Jubilation

"The timing is right now, we are both very, very happy." These words, uttered by Prince William during the announcement of his engagement to Catherine Middleton, reverberated across the United Kingdom and beyond, igniting a wave of excitement and anticipation. The engagement, revealed to the world on November 16, 2010, marked not just the union of two individuals, but the beginning of a new era for the British monarchy.

A Kenyan Proposal: Romance in the Wild

The story of the engagement itself reads like a fairy tale set against the backdrop of the African wilderness. Prince William chose to propose during a private trip to Kenya, a country that held profound significance for him. Kenya was not only a place of natural beauty but also a sanctuary where William could escape the constant scrutiny of royal life.

The proposal took place at Rutundu Cabin, a remote alpine lodge perched on the slopes of Mount Kenya, within the expansive Lewa Wildlife Conservancy. This secluded retreat, accessible only by helicopter or a grueling 15-kilometer hike, offered the couple the privacy they craved.

William had planned the moment meticulously. After a day spent fishing for rainbow trout in the nearby lake, the couple returned to their cabin. As the sun began to set, painting the sky in hues of orange and pink, William led Catherine out onto the wooden deck overlooking the wilderness. There, with the majestic Mount Kenya as their witness, he got down on one knee and asked Catherine to be his wife.

The ring he presented was a piece of history itself - the sapphire and diamond engagement ring that had once graced the finger of his mother, Diana, Princess of Wales. This 18-carat white gold ring, featuring a 12-carat oval Ceylon sapphire surrounded by 14 round diamonds, was more than just a beautiful piece of jewelry. It was a poignant symbol, a way for William to include his late mother in this pivotal moment of his life.

Catherine, overcome with emotion, said yes. Later, she would describe the proposal as *"very romantic"* and *"very personal,"* emphasizing William's thoughtfulness in choosing such a meaningful location and ring.

The Announcement: A Nation Rejoices

The news of the engagement, when it broke, sent ripples of joy across the United Kingdom and beyond. On November 16, 2010, the couple appeared before the world's media at St. James's Palace in London. Catherine, resplendent in a sapphire blue Issa dress that complemented her engagement ring, stood beside her prince, both radiating happiness.

During the press conference, the couple shared insights into their relationship and the proposal. William spoke of his decision to use his mother's ring, saying, *"It's very special to me. It was my way of making sure my mother didn't miss out on today and the excitement."* Catherine added, *"It's beautiful. I just hope I look after it. It's very, very special."*

The announcement was met with an outpouring of good wishes from all quarters. Queen Elizabeth II and Prince Philip expressed their delight, with the Queen saying she was "absolutely delighted" for the couple. Prince Charles and the Duchess of Cornwall also shared their joy, with Charles quipping, "They've been practicing long enough."

The public reaction was equally enthusiastic. People lined the streets outside Buckingham Palace, waving flags and cheering. Social media platforms were flooded with congratulatory messages, and news outlets around the world led with the story. The engagement represented not just a personal milestone for William and Catherine, but a moment of national celebration and unity.

Preparation for Royal Life: Catherine's Journey

For Catherine, the engagement marked the beginning of her official journey into royal life. While she had been in the public eye as William's girlfriend for several years, her new role as a future member of the royal family brought with it a new level of scrutiny and responsibility.

In the months following the engagement, Catherine embarked on an intensive period of preparation. She received lessons in royal protocol, etiquette, and the constitutional role of the monarchy. She also began to familiarize herself with the numerous charities and organizations she would be expected to support as a royal.

One of the most significant steps in Catherine's preparation was her confirmation into the Church of England. On March 10, 2011, in a private ceremony at

St. James's Palace, Catherine was confirmed by the Bishop of London. This spiritual commitment was seen as an important step, given the monarch's role as the Supreme Governor of the Church of England.

Catherine approached these preparations with characteristic grace and determination. Those close to her noted her commitment to learning and her genuine desire to serve in her new role. William was said to be a constant source of support, guiding her through the intricacies of royal life and standing by her side at public appearances.

The Wedding Plans: A Royal Affair in the Making

As the engagement was celebrated, attention quickly turned to the wedding plans. The date was set for April 29, 2011, and the venue chosen was the historic Westminster Abbey. This choice was steeped in royal tradition, being the site of countless coronations and royal weddings throughout history.

The planning of a royal wedding is no small feat, and a dedicated team was assembled to handle the myriad details. From the guest list (which would eventually include 1,900 people) to the music, flowers, and security arrangements, every aspect was carefully considered and debated.

One of the most talked-about elements of the wedding was, of course, Catherine's dress. Designed by Sarah Burton for Alexander McQueen, the dress was kept a closely guarded secret until the wedding day. Speculation ran rife, with fashion experts and royal watchers alike offering their predictions and opinions.

The couple was determined to make the wedding, despite its grandeur, a reflection of their personal tastes and values. They chose to have a charity gift fund in lieu of a traditional wedding list, allowing well-wishers to donate to causes close to their hearts. They also insisted on including personal touches, such as having Catherine's sister Pippa as maid of honor and William's brother Harry as best man.

Public Interest and Media Frenzy

The months leading up to the wedding saw an unprecedented level of public interest and media coverage. Catherine, in particular, found herself at the center of intense scrutiny. Every aspect of her life, from her fashion choices to her family background, was dissected and analyzed.

The media dubbed the phenomenon *"Kate-mania."* Magazines and newspapers devoted countless pages to stories about Catherine, and television networks planned extensive coverage of the wedding. Merchandise bearing the couple's image flooded the market, from mugs and tea towels to more unusual items like pizza cutters and garden gnomes.

While the attention was often overwhelming, Catherine handled it with remarkable poise. She maintained a dignified silence in the face of intrusive questions and continued to support William in his royal duties. Her grace under pressure earned her admiration from many quarters and set the tone for her future role as a royal.

The Wedding Day: A Fairy Tale Come to Life

When April 29, 2011, finally arrived, it seemed as if the entire world was watching. The day was declared a public holiday in the UK, and hundreds of thousands of well-wishers lined the streets of London, hoping to catch a glimpse of the royal couple.

Westminster Abbey was transformed into a veritable forest, with six English field maples and two hornbeams lining the aisle. The scent of lily of the valley, Catherine's favorite flower, filled the air. As the guests took their seats, the anticipation was palpable.

The moment everyone had been waiting for arrived when Catherine stepped out of the Rolls-Royce Phantom VI at the Abbey's Great West Door. Her dress, finally revealed, was a masterpiece of British craftsmanship. The lace appliqué bodice and sleeves were made by the Royal School of Needlework, and the full skirt was designed to echo an opening flower. On her head, she wore a Cartier halo tiara, lent to her by the Queen.

As Catherine walked down the aisle on her father's arm, a collective gasp could be heard. William, waiting at the altar in his red Irish Guards uniform, whispered to her,

"You look beautiful." The ceremony that followed was a perfect blend of tradition and personal touches, including readings by Catherine's brother James and a homily by the Bishop of London.

After exchanging vows and rings, the newly married Duke and Duchess of Cambridge (as they were now styled) emerged from the Abbey to the pealing of bells and the cheers of thousands. They rode in a 1902 State Landau carriage to Buckingham Palace, waving to the crowds lining the Mall.

The iconic balcony appearance at Buckingham Palace provided one of the most memorable moments of the day. As William and Catherine stepped out, the roar from the crowd was deafening. The couple shared two kisses, to the delight of onlookers, before watching a flypast by the Royal Air Force.

A New Chapter Begins

The wedding marked not just the union of William and Catherine, but the beginning of a new chapter in the story of the British monarchy. As the couple embarked on their life together, they faced the dual challenges of building a marriage and fulfilling their royal duties.

In the years that followed, William and Catherine would go on to have three children - Prince George, Princess Charlotte, and Prince Louis. They would take on increasing responsibilities within the royal family, championing causes close to their hearts and representing the monarchy both at home and abroad.

Throughout it all, the love and partnership that was so evident on their wedding day has remained a constant. William and Catherine's relationship, from their engagement to their marriage and beyond, stands as a testament to the power of love, commitment, and shared purpose.

As we look back on the fairy tale engagement and wedding of William and Catherine, we see more than just a beautiful love story. We see the foundations being laid for the future of the British monarchy - a future built on the ideals of service, duty, and compassion, embodied in the grace, strength, and humanity of Catherine, the future Queen of Wales.

Life as the Princess of Wales

"To be the best version of yourself, you must bring your whole self to the table - your experiences, your passions, your dreams." - Catherine, Princess of Wales

Catherine's transition into her role as Princess of Wales marked a significant evolution in her royal journey. This prestigious title, previously held by Diana, Princess of Wales, came with immense responsibility and public scrutiny. Catherine has approached this role with grace, determination, and a clear vision for how she wishes to make a difference.

From the moment she stepped into this role, Catherine has been acutely aware of its historical significance and the expectations placed upon her. She has often spoken about the honor and responsibility she feels in carrying forward the legacy of those who came before her, while also carving out her own unique path.

Catherine's approach to royal life has been characterized by a blend of tradition and modernity. She respects and upholds the protocols and traditions of the monarchy, but also brings a fresh, contemporary perspective to her role. This balance has been evident in everything from her fashion choices to her selection of causes to champion.

One of the hallmarks of Catherine's tenure as Princess of Wales has been her commitment to early childhood development. This focus stems from her understanding that the early years of a child's life are crucial in shaping their future. Her dedication to this cause has been evident in numerous initiatives and projects she has spearheaded.

Public Duties and Charitable Work

Catherine's charitable work is extensive and diverse, reflecting her wide-ranging interests and her desire to make a tangible difference in people's lives. Her approach to philanthropy is hands-on and personal, often involving direct engagement with the people and communities she aims to help.

Early Childhood Development

At the heart of Catherine's charitable work is her commitment to early childhood development. In 2021, she launched The Royal Foundation Centre for Early Childhood, a landmark initiative aimed at raising awareness of and promoting action on the extraordinary impact of the early years.

The Centre focuses on three key areas: research, collaboration, and awareness-raising. It brings together experts from across disciplines to find innovative solutions to challenges in early childhood development. Catherine has been deeply involved in every aspect of the Centre's work, from its conception to its ongoing projects.

One of the Centre's significant projects is the *"5 Big Questions"* survey, which Catherine spearheaded. This nationwide survey aimed to spark a national conversation about the importance of early childhood and to gather data to inform future initiatives. The survey received over 500,000 responses, making it the largest survey of its kind in UK history.

Catherine's work in this area extends beyond the Centre. She regularly visits nurseries, schools, and family support centers across the UK, engaging directly with children, parents, and caregivers. These visits are not mere photo opportunities; Catherine uses them to listen, learn, and gain insights that inform her work.

In one particularly memorable visit to a London nursery, Catherine rolled up her sleeves and joined the children in their play activities. She spent time finger painting, reading stories, and even joining in a game of hide-and-seek. The staff noted her genuine enthusiasm and her ability to connect with the children on their level.

Mental Health Advocacy

Another key focus of Catherine's charitable work is mental health, particularly among young people. Along with Prince William and Prince Harry, she launched the Heads Together campaign in 2016, aimed at ending the stigma around mental health.

Catherine has been particularly vocal about the importance of mental health support for new mothers. She has shared her own experiences of the challenges of motherhood, breaking down barriers and encouraging open conversations about postpartum mental health.

In 2020, Catherine launched the *"Shout"* text messaging support service, a 24/7 crisis line for people struggling with mental health issues. She has been known to volunteer on the service herself, demonstrating her hands-on approach to her charitable work.

During a visit to a mental health charity in Liverpool, Catherine spent time talking with young people who had benefited from the organization's services. One young woman, Sarah, later shared how Catherine's warmth and genuine interest had made her feel truly heard. *"She wasn't just asking questions for the sake of it,"* Sarah said. "You could tell she really cared and wanted to understand our experiences."

Sports and Physical Activity

Catherine's love for sports and her belief in its power to promote both physical and mental wellbeing is another cornerstone of her charitable work. She is patron of several sports-related charities and regularly participates in sporting events to raise awareness and funds.

In 2022, Catherine launched a campaign to promote the importance of physical activity for young children. The initiative included a series of fun, accessible exercises that families could do together at home or in local parks. Catherine herself demonstrated some of the exercises in a video that went viral, showcasing her ability to connect with people through relatable, everyday activities.

During the 2023 Wimbledon Championships, Catherine, as patron of the All England Lawn Tennis Club, took part in a tennis clinic for underprivileged children. She spent the afternoon playing tennis with the children, offering encouragement and tips. One of the coaches present noted, "She has a natural way with kids. They were all a bit star-struck at first, but within minutes, she had them laughing and fully engaged in the game."

Arts and Culture

Catherine's appreciation for the arts and her belief in their power to enrich lives and bring communities together is reflected in her patronage of several cultural institutions. She has been a strong advocate for art therapy and the use of creative activities to support mental health and wellbeing.

In 2021, Catherine launched a nationwide photography competition called "Hold Still," inviting people to submit photographs that captured their experiences during the

COVID-19 pandemic. The project was a resounding success, receiving over 31,000 submissions. Catherine personally curated the final selection of 100 portraits, which were displayed in a virtual exhibition and later published in a book.

The *"Hold Still"* project exemplified Catherine's ability to connect with people on a personal level, even amid the constraints of a global pandemic. She conducted video calls with some of the photographers whose work was selected, listening to their stories and sharing her own reflections on the power of photography to capture human experiences.

Environmental Conservation

In recent years, Catherine has increasingly turned her attention to environmental issues, particularly focusing on how environmental degradation impacts children's wellbeing. She has become a vocal advocate for nature-based learning and the importance of connecting children with the natural world.

In 2023, Catherine launched the *"Nature Nurtures"* initiative, a program designed to create more opportunities for urban children to experience and learn from nature. The initiative includes the creation of natural play areas in urban settings, school gardening programs, and wilderness therapy sessions for children struggling with mental health issues.

During the launch of this initiative, Catherine spent a day with a group of inner-city children on a nature walk in Richmond Park. She joined them in activities like bark rubbing, bird watching, and planting wildflowers. One of the children, 8-year-old Zara, later said, "I never knew there was so much to see and do in nature. The Princess showed us how to listen for different bird calls. She knows so much about nature!"

Behind the Scenes: Catherine's Approach to Royal Life

While Catherine's public duties and charitable work are well-documented, it's the behind-the-scenes moments and personal anecdotes that truly reveal her character and approach to royal life.

Catherine is known for her meticulous preparation for her engagements. She often spends hours researching the organizations she's visiting and the issues they're addressing. This thoroughness was evident during a visit to a children's hospice in 2022. The staff were impressed by her in-depth knowledge of palliative care for children and her thoughtful questions about their specific challenges.

Despite her royal status, Catherine is known for her down-to-earth nature and ability to put people at ease. During a visit to a women's prison in 2021, she sat down for a informal chat with a group of inmates. One of the women later shared, "She didn't make us feel judged. She listened to our stories and spoke to us like we were just normal people having a conversation."

Catherine's hands-on approach extends to her office work as well. She is known to be deeply involved in the planning and execution of her initiatives. During the development of the Early Childhood Centre, she regularly attended meetings with researchers and child development experts, actively participating in discussions and contributing ideas.

Her staff often comment on her work ethic and attention to detail. One aide shared an anecdote about Catherine staying up late to personally write thank-you notes to everyone who had contributed to a charity event she had organized. *"She believes in the power of personal touch,"* the aide explained. *"She wants people to know that their efforts are truly appreciated."*

Catherine's role as a mother is central to her approach to royal duties. She often draws on her experiences as a parent in her work, using them to connect with other parents and to inform her initiatives. During a visit to a parent support group, she shared her own struggles with balancing work and family life, earning nods of recognition from the other parents present.

Despite the demands of her role, Catherine is known to prioritize her family life. She has spoken about the importance of having dinner together as a family and maintaining as normal a life as possible for her children. This balance between her public duties and private life is something she works hard to maintain.

Catherine's sense of humor and playful nature often shine through in her interactions. During a visit to a children's hospital in 2023, she joined in a tea party with young patients, donning a tiara and feather boa provided by the children. The nurses noted how her willingness to be silly and play along brought joy to the children and their families.

Her ability to remain calm under pressure has been noted by many who work with her. During a live television interview about her early childhood work, the studio lights unexpectedly went out. Without missing a beat, Catherine laughed it off and continued the interview in the dim emergency lighting, turning what could have been an awkward moment into a charming one.

Catherine's approach to fashion has also been a significant aspect of her public role. While she is known for her elegant style, she also uses her wardrobe choices strategically to support British designers, highlight sustainable fashion, and sometimes to convey subtle messages. For instance, during a state visit to Ireland, she wore green as a diplomatic nod to the host country.

In her role as Princess of Wales, Catherine has shown a remarkable ability to balance tradition with modernity, formality with approachability, and duty with genuine passion. Her unique blend of grace, empathy, and determination has earned her respect and admiration, not just in the UK, but around the world.

As she continues to grow in her role, Catherine's impact on the monarchy and on the causes she champions is likely to be profound and long-lasting. Her journey as the Princess of Wales is not just about fulfilling a royal role, but about using her position to make a real difference in people's lives. Through her work, she is shaping the future of the monarchy and leaving her own unique mark on the role of Princess of Wales.

Strength in Adversity

"Courage does not always roar. Sometimes courage is the quiet voice at the end of the day saying, 'I will try again tomorrow.'" - Mary Anne Radmacher

When public figures face health crises, it often becomes a defining moment not just in their personal lives, but in their public roles as well. For someone in Catherine's position as a senior member of the British Royal Family, any significant health challenge would likely have far-reaching implications, affecting not only her immediate family but also her public duties and the public's perception of the monarchy.

Health Challenges for Public Figures

Public figures, especially those in roles as visible and scrutinized as the British Royal Family, often face unique challenges when dealing with health issues. There's a delicate balance to be struck between maintaining privacy and meeting the public's expectation for transparency about the health of their leaders and representatives.

In the case of a serious diagnosis like cancer, the impact would be profound and multifaceted. The immediate focus would be on treatment and recovery, but there would also be considerations about how to communicate the news to the public, how to manage public duties and appearances, and how to support the family through a challenging time.

"Life doesn't get easier or more forgiving, we get stronger and more resilient." These words, though not spoken by Catherine herself, encapsulate the spirit of resilience and strength she has demonstrated in the face of adversity. In January 2024, Catherine, Princess of Wales, faced a life-altering challenge when she was

diagnosed with cancer following major abdominal surgery. This unexpected turn of events would test her resolve, the support of her family, and the adaptability of her royal duties.

Diagnosis and Treatment Journey

For any individual, a cancer diagnosis is a life-altering event. For a public figure like Catherine, it would likely involve a complex interplay of personal health management and public communication strategies.

The journey typically begins with initial symptoms or routine screenings leading to further tests. In many cases, what starts as a seemingly routine medical procedure can lead to unexpected findings. For example, during abdominal surgery, it's not uncommon for doctors to conduct biopsies on any suspicious tissues they encounter. These biopsies can sometimes reveal cancerous cells that weren't apparent in initial scans or tests.

Once a diagnosis is confirmed, treatment plans are developed based on the type and stage of cancer. For many types of cancer, treatment often involves a combination of approaches, which may include surgery, chemotherapy, radiation therapy, or newer targeted therapies and immunotherapies.

Preventive or adjuvant chemotherapy is a common approach for many types of cancer, especially when there's a risk of recurrence or spread. This type of treatment is given after the primary tumor has been removed surgically, with the goal of destroying any remaining cancer cells that might be present in the body but are too small to detect.

Catherine's journey began with a planned abdominal surgery at the London Clinic in January 2024. Initially, the surgery was thought to be for a non-cancerous condition, and Kensington Palace announced that she would spend two weeks recovering in the hospital.

However, the post-operative tests revealed a shocking truth: cancer had been present. This diagnosis came as a *"huge shock"* to Catherine and her family, particularly her husband, Prince William, and their three children, Prince George, Princess Charlotte, and Prince Louis.

In a video message released on March 22, 2024, Catherine shared the details of her diagnosis and the subsequent treatment plan. She explained that her medical team advised her to undergo a course of preventive chemotherapy, also known as adjuvant chemotherapy, to reduce the risk of cancer recurrence.

The Treatment Journey: Early Stages of Preventive Chemotherapy

Preventive chemotherapy, or adjuvant chemotherapy, is a treatment administered after primary treatments like surgery to target microscopic cancer cells that may remain in the body. This proactive approach aims to weaken the chances of cancer returning, thereby improving the patient's prognosis.

Catherine began her chemotherapy treatment in late February 2024, marking the beginning of a challenging but crucial phase in her health journey. The early stages of treatment were characterized by a mix of physical and emotional challenges, as she had to balance her recovery from major surgery with the onset of chemotherapy.

The process of undergoing chemotherapy is grueling, involving multiple sessions over several months. Catherine's treatment plan was tailored to her specific condition, though the exact details of her cancer diagnosis were not disclosed to the public.

Impact on Family

A cancer diagnosis affects not just the individual, but the entire family. For Catherine, Prince William, and their children, it would be a time of significant adjustment and emotional challenge.

Explaining a serious illness to children is always difficult, and the approach would likely vary depending on the ages of the children. Prince George, being older, might be given more detailed information, while the younger children might receive a simpler explanation focused on reassurance and maintaining their routine as much as possible.

The diagnosis and subsequent treatment had a profound impact on Catherine's family, particularly her children. Explaining such a serious health issue to young children is a delicate task, requiring sensitivity and honesty.

Catherine and Prince William took the time to explain the situation to their children in a way that was appropriate for their ages. This process was not only emotionally challenging but also crucial in reassuring them that their mother was receiving the best care possible.

The couple's approach to managing this difficult conversation reflects their commitment to their family's well-being. By being open and supportive, they aimed to minimize the anxiety and uncertainty that such news could bring to their young family.

Impact on Royal Duties

Catherine's health crisis necessitated a temporary absence from her official royal duties. This decision was made to ensure she could focus on her recovery and treatment without the added pressure of public engagements.

A health crisis of this magnitude would inevitably impact Catherine's ability to perform her royal duties, at least in the short term. The extent of this impact would depend on the specifics of her treatment plan and her overall health status.

The royal family and Kensington Palace were supportive of her decision, understanding the importance of her health and well-being during this critical period. Prince William and other members of the royal family stepped in to cover some of her engagements, demonstrating the family's solidarity and commitment to their duties.

The palace communications team would play a crucial role in managing public expectations and providing appropriate updates. They would need to balance the public's interest and concern with Catherine's right to privacy during her treatment and recovery.

Other members of the royal family would likely step in to cover some of Catherine's scheduled appearances and patronages. This could include increased public roles for other senior royals, potentially including Princess Anne, the Duchess of Edinburgh, or even Prince William taking on additional engagements.

Resilience and Support

Throughout such a challenging time, Catherine's resilience would be put to the test. However, based on her past behavior and public persona, it's likely that she would approach this challenge with the same grace and determination she's shown in other aspects of her royal life.

Public figures who have faced health crises often speak about finding strength they didn't know they had. For many, the experience becomes a catalyst for personal growth and can even reshape their public role and the causes they champion.

The support of Prince William would be crucial during this time. Royal couples often speak about the strength they draw from their partnership, especially during challenging times. William's own experiences with his mother's illness and loss would likely inform his approach to supporting Catherine and their children.

Throughout this challenging time, Catherine's resilience and the support she received from her family were paramount. Prince William was a constant source of comfort and strength, standing by her side as she navigated the complexities of her treatment.

King Charles III and Queen Camilla also offered their love and support, remaining in close contact with Catherine and her family. The royal family's unity and support were evident in their public statements, with King Charles expressing his pride in Catherine's courage and the family's collective resolve to face this challenge together.

The public reaction to Catherine's diagnosis was one of sympathy and support. UK Prime Minister Rishi Sunak praised her bravery, and the White House extended their wishes for her full recovery. Even Prince Harry and Meghan, Duchess of Sussex, expressed their support, highlighting the broader sense of solidarity within the royal family and beyond.

Public Support and Privacy

In situations like this, there's often an outpouring of public support. Messages of goodwill from the public, other public figures, and world leaders would likely flood in. Managing this public interest while maintaining necessary privacy would be a delicate balance for the palace communications team.

There might be decisions to be made about how much information to share with the public. In recent years, the royal family has generally taken a more open approach to health issues, recognizing the public's concern and the potential to raise awareness for important health issues. However, the specific details shared would likely be carefully considered to protect Catherine's privacy and that of her family.

Long-term Impact and Legacy

A health crisis of this nature often has long-lasting impacts, not just on the individual but on their public role and legacy. For many public figures who have faced serious illnesses, their experiences become part of their public narrative and can shape their future work and advocacy.

For Catherine, this experience could potentially influence her future charitable work. Many individuals who survive cancer become advocates for cancer research, early detection, or improved patient care. Given Catherine's existing focus on health and wellbeing, particularly mental health, this could become an additional area of focus in her charitable work.

The experience could also potentially impact the public's perception of Catherine and the wider royal family. Often, seeing public figures navigate personal challenges can make them seem more relatable and human to the public. It could strengthen the public's empathy and support for the royal family.

In terms of the monarchy as an institution, how the family handles such a crisis can have significant implications. The royal family's ability to adapt to challenges and continue their duties even in difficult times is often seen as a testament to the resilience of the monarchy as an institution.

Personal Growth and Perspective

Many individuals who face serious health challenges speak about how the experience changes their perspective on life. For someone in Catherine's position, this could manifest in various ways. It might influence her priorities in terms of balancing public duties with family life. It could impact her approach to her role, perhaps leading to an even greater focus on health-related causes or a desire to use her platform to make a more immediate impact.

There might also be changes in her personal style or public persona. Many people who go through serious illnesses speak about feeling less concerned with superficial matters and more focused on what truly matters to them. For a public figure like Catherine, even subtle changes in demeanor or focus can be noticeable and influential.

The experience could also potentially bring about a new level of openness. While the royal family traditionally maintains a certain level of privacy, Catherine might choose to speak more openly about her experiences as a way of connecting with others who have faced similar challenges and raising awareness about important health issues.

Family Dynamics

A health crisis often leads to shifts in family dynamics. For the Cambridge family, this could mean closer bonds forged through shared adversity. The children, even at their young ages, might develop new levels of empathy and understanding. Prince George, as the oldest, might take on more responsibility or show increased maturity.

For Prince William, supporting Catherine through this challenge could bring about personal growth as well. Balancing the roles of supportive spouse, father, and future king during a family health crisis would be a significant test of his character and abilities.

The experience could also potentially bring Catherine closer to other members of the royal family who have faced health challenges. Shared experiences often create strong bonds, and this could lead to new alliances or collaborations within the family.

Public Appearances and the Road to Recovery

Despite her ongoing treatment, Catherine made a determined effort to return to public life. Her first public appearance after the diagnosis was at the 2024 Trooping the

Colour in June, where she attended the event while still undergoing treatment.

This appearance was a testament to her strength and commitment to her royal duties. In a letter released by Kensington Palace, Catherine mentioned that she was still undergoing treatment but was focused on making a full recovery. Her occasional appearances over the following months were carefully managed to ensure she did not overexert herself while continuing her treatment.

Catherine's journey through cancer diagnosis and treatment is a story of resilience, strength, and the unwavering support of her family. As she continues to face the challenges of her health crisis, her determination and grace serve as an inspiration to many. This chapter in her life underscores the themes of strength and adversity that define her biography, highlighting her ability to confront and overcome even the most daunting obstacles.

The road to recovery is long and arduous, but with the support of her loved ones and the broader public, Catherine remains steadfast in her resolve. Her story is a powerful reminder that even in the darkest moments, there is always hope and the potential for healing and recovery. As she moves forward, Catherine's journey will undoubtedly continue to inspire and captivate, reflecting the enduring spirit of a woman who embodies the very essence of grace, secrets, and strength.

Media Coverage and Public Perception

The media coverage of a royal health crisis is typically intense and can be challenging to manage. The palace communications team would need to strike a balance between providing enough information to satisfy public concern and protecting Catherine's privacy.

There might be decisions to be made about whether to allow any media coverage of Catherine's treatment journey. Some public figures choose to document their experiences as a way of raising awareness, while others prefer to keep the details private.

The way the media and public respond to Catherine's health challenge could also potentially impact public perception of the media itself. There's often a public debate about the appropriate level of scrutiny for public figures during personal crises.

Global Impact

Given the global prominence of the British Royal Family, Catherine's health journey would likely resonate far beyond the UK. It could potentially impact diplomatic engagements and international relations, particularly if planned overseas visits need to be postponed or canceled.

There might also be a global conversation about health issues, particularly if Catherine chooses to use her experience to advocate for certain health causes. The royal family has a history of bringing attention to health issues, from Prince Harry's work on mental health to Prince Charles' advocacy for complementary medicine.

Long-term Royal Planning

A serious health challenge for a key member of the royal family would likely prompt some long-term planning discussions within the institution. This might include conversations about succession planning, distribution of royal duties, and how to ensure the continuity of the monarchy's work in various scenarios.

For Catherine personally, it might lead to discussions about her future role and responsibilities. There might be considerations about how to balance her health needs with her royal duties in the long term.

Charitable Work and Advocacy

As mentioned earlier, Catherine's charitable work could be significantly influenced by her health experiences. Many public figures who have faced health challenges become powerful advocates for related causes.

This could manifest in various ways:

- Becoming a patron of cancer-related charities
- Using her platform to promote cancer awareness and early detection
- Advocating for improvements in cancer care and support for patients and families

- ❖ Sharing her personal story to inspire and support others facing similar challenges
- ❖ Incorporating her experiences into her existing work on mental health, recognizing the psychological impact of serious illnesses

Catherine's unique position as a senior royal could allow her to bring significant attention and resources to these causes. Her personal experience could lend authenticity and depth to her advocacy work.

Family Life and Parenting

A health crisis often leads to shifts in family dynamics and parenting approaches. For Catherine and William, this experience could influence how they approach parenting and the values they emphasize with their children.

They might place an even greater emphasis on health and wellbeing in their family life. This could include more open conversations about health, encouraging healthy lifestyles, and fostering resilience in their children. The experience might also impact how they prepare their children, particularly Prince George, for their future roles. It could lead to discussions about the importance of health and self-care even in positions of great responsibility.

Public Speaking and Engagements

As Catherine returns to public duties, her speeches and the causes she chooses to highlight might reflect her experiences. Many public figures find that personal challenges give them a new voice and perspective in their public roles.

She might choose to speak more personally in her engagements, sharing aspects of her journey to connect with others who have faced health challenges. This could bring a new depth and authenticity to her public persona.

There might also be a shift in the types of engagements she undertakes. She might choose to focus more on hospital visits, medical research facilities, or organizations supporting patients and families dealing with serious illnesses.

Fashion and Public Image

While it might seem trivial in the face of serious health challenges, for a public figure like Catherine, even changes in personal style can be significant and noticed by the public.

There might be practical considerations in her fashion choices during and after treatment. Many cancer patients, for example, experience changes in their appearance or comfort levels that influence their clothing choices.

More profoundly, her experiences might influence her overall public image. Many people find that facing a serious illness changes their priorities and how they want to present themselves to the world. For Catherine, this could manifest in subtle but noticeable ways in her public appearances and interactions.

Technology and Treatment

Given the royal family's resources and influence, Catherine's treatment journey could potentially involve cutting-edge medical technologies and treatments. While maintaining medical privacy, there might be opportunities to highlight advancements in cancer treatment and care.

This could dovetail with the royal family's existing interests in innovation and technology. There might be opportunities to support and highlight medical research and technological advancements in healthcare.

Mental Health Advocacy

Given Catherine's existing work in mental health, her experiences could bring a new dimension to this advocacy. She might choose to highlight the mental health challenges that come with serious physical health diagnoses.

This could include addressing issues like:

❖ The psychological impact of a cancer diagnosis
❖ Mental health support for patients and families during treatment
❖ The importance of psychological care as part of holistic cancer treatment
❖ Strategies for maintaining mental wellbeing during health challenges

Her personal experiences could make her an even more powerful advocate in this area, potentially leading to increased resources and attention for mental health support in medical settings.

Legacy and Future Impact

How Catherine handles this health challenge and its aftermath could become a significant part of her legacy as a royal figure. It could influence how she's perceived by the public and how she shapes her role in the years to come.

This experience could potentially make her an even more relatable and respected figure, someone who has faced a challenge many people fear and emerged with grace and strength. It could cement her position as a role model and influential public figure beyond her royal title.

In the long term, this chapter in Catherine's life could have far-reaching impacts on public health awareness, cancer research funding, and support for patients and families facing similar challenges. Her journey could become a powerful narrative in the ongoing story of the British monarchy, demonstrating its ability to connect with the public through shared human experiences.

As Catherine moves forward, balancing her health needs, family life, and royal duties, she has the opportunity to redefine what it means to be a modern royal. Her experiences could shape not just her own role, but potentially influence the future direction of the monarchy as an institution that remains relevant and connected to the people it serves.

Public Appearances and Style

"Fashion is the armor to survive the reality of everyday life." - Bill Cunningham

Catherine, the Princess of Wales, has long been recognized as a fashion icon whose style choices are closely watched and often emulated around the world. Her approach to fashion has always been a careful balance of elegance, appropriateness for her royal role, and personal expression.

From her earliest days in the public eye, Catherine has shown a keen understanding of the power of fashion in shaping public perception and communicating messages without words. Her style evolution over the years reflects not just changing trends, but also her growing confidence in her royal role and her personal growth.

Early Style Evolution

When Catherine first entered the public spotlight as Prince William's girlfriend, her style was that of a typical British university student - casual, comfortable, and youthful. As her relationship with William became more serious and her public profile grew, her style began to evolve.

During her engagement and in the early years of her marriage, Catherine's style was characterized by a mix of high street and designer fashion. She became known for wearing accessible brands like Zara and Reiss, often causing items to sell out within hours of her being photographed in them - a phenomenon that became known as the *"Kate Effect."*

This approach endeared her to the public, presenting her as relatable and down-to-earth despite her royal status. At the same time, she began incorporating more high-end designer pieces into her wardrobe for formal occasions, signaling her transition into her role as a future queen.

Developing a Royal Wardrobe

As Catherine settled into her role as the Duchess of Cambridge (her title before becoming Princess of Wales), her style became more polished and sophisticated. She developed a signature look that typically included:

1. Tailored coats and coat dresses: These became a staple of her public appearance wardrobe, offering a smart and put-together look that worked well for a variety of engagements.

2. Fitted dresses: Catherine often chose dresses that accentuated her slim figure while remaining modest and appropriate for her role.

3. Subtle patterns and solid colors: While she occasionally wore bold prints, Catherine often opted for solid colors or subtle patterns, allowing her to stand out without overshadowing the purpose of her appearances.

4. Classic pumps: Her footwear choices were often classic court shoes in neutral colors, providing a sophisticated finish to her outfits.

5. Meaningful jewelry: Catherine frequently wore pieces with significance, including items that belonged to Princess Diana and pieces that represented the countries or organizations she was visiting.

Diplomatic Dressing

One area where Catherine's fashion choices have been particularly noteworthy is in her approach to diplomatic dressing. During royal tours and state visits, she often incorporates elements that pay tribute to the host country. This might include:

- ❖ Wearing the colors of the national flag
- ❖ Choosing designs by local designers
- ❖ Incorporating traditional patterns or motifs into her outfits
- ❖ Wearing jewelry gifted by or symbolic of the host nation

This thoughtful approach to fashion diplomacy has been widely praised and has helped to strengthen international relationships. It demonstrates Catherine's understanding of her role as a representative of the British monarchy and her respect for other cultures.

For example, during a visit to Pakistan in 2019, Catherine wore a number of outfits that paid homage to traditional Pakistani dress, including a stunning teal shalwar kameez by Catherine Walker. This choice was widely appreciated in Pakistan and demonstrated Catherine's cultural sensitivity and diplomatic acumen.

Championing British Fashion

While Catherine's wardrobe includes pieces from international designers, she has been a strong supporter of British fashion throughout her time as a royal. She frequently wears pieces by British designers such as Alexander McQueen, Jenny Packham, and Emilia Wickstead.

Her wedding dress, designed by Sarah Burton for Alexander McQueen, was a particularly significant moment for British fashion. The dress, with its long lace sleeves and fitted bodice, sparked a trend for similar styles in bridal fashion for years to come.

Catherine's support extends beyond well-established luxury brands. She has also worn pieces from up-and-coming British designers, giving them valuable exposure on the world stage. This support of the British fashion industry is an important part of her role as a senior royal, helping to promote British creativity and craftsmanship.

Balancing High-End and High Street

One of the most remarked-upon aspects of Catherine's style is her ability to mix high-end designer pieces with more affordable high street items. This approach has made her style feel accessible to many, while still maintaining the elegance expected of a royal.

For less formal engagements, Catherine might be seen in a dress from Zara or a blazer from Smythe, paired with designer accessories. For more formal occasions, she tends to favor custom-made pieces from her preferred British designers.

This high-low mix in her wardrobe has been a consistent feature of her style strategy, allowing her to connect with the public while still presenting an appropriately polished image for her role.

Recycling and Sustainability

Another notable aspect of Catherine's approach to fashion is her willingness to rewear outfits. In an era of increasing awareness about the environmental impact of fashion, Catherine's "outfit repeating" has been praised as a responsible and relatable choice.

She has been known to wear the same pieces multiple times, sometimes years apart, often styling them differently each time. This not only presents a more sustainable approach to fashion but also reinforces her image as practical and down-to-earth.

For example, a teal Jenny Packham gown that Catherine wore to an Olympic gala in 2012 made a reappearance, with slight modifications, at the Tusk Conservation Awards in 2018. Her ability to make a six-year-old dress look fresh and relevant was widely applauded.

Style for Different Roles

Catherine's wardrobe choices often reflect the different aspects of her royal role. Her style varies depending on the nature of the engagement:

1. Formal Events: For state dinners, film premieres, and other high-profile evening events, Catherine often chooses glamorous floor-length gowns. These are typically by British designers and often feature intricate detailing or embellishments.

2. Day Events: For daytime engagements, Catherine often opts for smart coat dresses or skirt suits. These offer a formal yet approachable look that works well for a

variety of events, from school visits to charity launches.

3. Sporting Events: When attending or participating in sporting events, Catherine's style becomes more casual. She's often seen in neat jeans or khakis paired with blazers or sporty jackets.

4. Family Occasions: For family-centric events like Christmas church services or children's parties, Catherine's style tends to be elegant but slightly more relaxed, often featuring softer silhouettes and warmer colors.

Influence on Fashion Industry

The *"Kate Effect"* - the phenomenon of items worn by Catherine selling out quickly - has had a significant impact on the fashion industry. Brands worn by Catherine often see a huge spike in sales and visibility.

This influence extends beyond individual items. Styles and trends popularized by Catherine often find their way into mainstream fashion. For example, her preference for sapphire blue (matching her famous engagement ring) has led to increased popularity of this color in fashion collections.

Catherine's influence has also extended to bridal fashion. Her wedding dress sparked a trend for lace sleeves and more modest, classic silhouettes in bridal wear that continued for years after her 2011 wedding.

Maternity Style

During her pregnancies, Catherine's maternity style garnered significant attention. She maintained her polished look throughout, favoring tailored coats and dresses that accommodated her changing figure while still looking elegant.

Her post-pregnancy appearances also attracted notice. Catherine's choice to appear in public shortly after giving birth, looking polished and put-together, sparked discussions about societal expectations of new mothers.

Hair and Beauty

While not strictly part of her fashion choices, Catherine's hair and makeup are integral parts of her overall style. Her glossy, bouncy blowouts have become something of a signature look, inspiring many to emulate her hairstyle.

Her makeup is typically natural-looking, with an emphasis on enhancing her features rather than dramatic or trendy looks. This classic approach to beauty complements her fashion choices and reinforces her image as timelessly elegant.

Jewelry Choices

Catherine's jewelry choices often carry special significance. She frequently wears pieces that belonged to Princess Diana, including her famous sapphire engagement ring. These choices serve as a touching tribute to William's mother and connect Catherine to royal history.

She also often wears jewelry that carries diplomatic significance, such as maple leaf brooches when visiting Canada or pieces gifted by other royal families.

For everyday wear, Catherine often chooses delicate, understated pieces. This approach allows her outfits to take center stage and maintains a relatable image.

Evolution of Style

Over the years, Catherine's style has evolved to reflect her growing confidence and changing role within the royal family. In her early years as a royal, her style was often described as safe and conservative. As she's grown more comfortable in her role, she's shown more willingness to take fashion risks and embrace bolder choices.

This evolution has been particularly noticeable in recent years. Catherine has experimented more with color, trying bolder hues and color combinations. She's also shown more variety in her silhouettes, moving beyond her signature fit-and-flare dresses to try wide-legged trousers, peplum jackets, and other more fashion-forward choices.

Style During the Pandemic

The global COVID-19 pandemic brought new challenges and considerations to Catherine's public appearances and style choices. During virtual engagements, she often chose brightly colored tops that looked good on camera and lifted spirits during a difficult time.

When in-person engagements resumed, Catherine's fashion choices often reflected the mood of the nation. She was seen rewearing familiar outfits more frequently, perhaps in recognition of the economic challenges many were facing.

The pandemic also saw Catherine embracing a more casual style for some engagements, particularly those related to healthcare or community support. This shift helped to convey approachability and solidarity during a time of national crisis.

Personal Expression Through Fashion

While Catherine's style is undoubtedly influenced by her royal role, it also serves as a form of personal expression. Her choices often reflect her personal interests and the causes she champions.

For example, her support of environmental causes is reflected in her choice to wear sustainable brands or to rewear outfits. Her interest in children's early years development is sometimes mirrored in playful, child-friendly elements in her outfits for engagements related to this cause.

Catherine's style also reflects her personal growth and increasing confidence in her role. As she's taken on more senior responsibilities within the royal family, her fashion choices have become more assured and authoritative, while still maintaining her signature elegance.

The Power of Fashion in Royal Storytelling

Fashion has long been an important tool for royals to communicate messages and shape public perception. Catherine's skillful use of fashion as a form of non-verbal communication has been one of the defining features of her royal career.

Her style choices often reflect the tone and purpose of her engagements. For somber occasions, she chooses muted colors and conservative styles. For joyful events, she might opt for brighter colors or more playful designs. This thoughtful approach to dressing demonstrates her understanding of the power of visual messaging in her role.

Catherine's fashion choices also help to shape the narrative around the modern monarchy. Her mix of high-end and high street fashion, her outfit repeating, and her support of British brands all contribute to an image of a monarchy that is both regal and relatable, steeped in tradition yet in touch with contemporary life.

Looking to the Future

As Catherine continues in her role as Princess of Wales and looks ahead to her future as Queen Consort, her style will likely continue to evolve. It will be interesting to see how she balances the weight of tradition with the need for the monarchy to remain relevant and relatable.

Given her track record, it's likely that Catherine will continue to use fashion as a powerful tool for diplomacy, personal expression, and connecting with the public. Her style choices will undoubtedly continue to be closely watched and influential, both within the UK and around the world.

As she takes on more senior roles and represents the monarchy at the highest levels, we may see a further evolution in her style. This could involve more regal and formal choices for state occasions, balanced with her trademark relatability for less formal engagements.

Whatever direction her style takes, it's clear that Catherine's fashion choices will remain an important part of her public persona and her role within the royal family. Her ability to use fashion as a form of silent diplomacy, personal expression, and public connection has been one of the defining features of her time as a royal, and will likely continue to be so in the years to come.

Secrets of the Royal Family: Traditions, Protocols, and Family Dynamics

"The British monarchy is like a great big machine. It needs oiling, it needs looking after, and it needs to be driven somewhere." These words, spoken by Queen Elizabeth II, encapsulate the intricate and often mysterious world of the British royal family. Behind the grandeur and pageantry lies a complex web of traditions, protocols, and family dynamics that are not commonly known to the public. This chapter delves into these intriguing aspects, providing a deeper understanding of the royal family's inner workings.

Royal Traditions: A Legacy of Customs and Practices

The British royal family is steeped in tradition, with many customs and practices passed down through generations. One of the most enduring traditions is the annual gathering at Sandringham House in Norfolk for Christmas. This tradition, which dates back to the 19th century, involves the entire royal family coming together to celebrate the holiday, exchange gifts, and attend church services.

Another significant tradition is the attendance at Royal Ascot, a prestigious horse racing event. The royal family has been associated with Royal Ascot for centuries, and it remains a highlight of their social calendar. The event is marked by the traditional procession of carriages from Windsor Castle to the Ascot grounds, a spectacle that has been a part of British royal life for over 200 years.

Royal Protocols: Rules and Etiquette

Royal life is governed by a strict set of protocols that dictate everything from how to greet the monarch to what to wear at formal events. One of the most well-known protocols is the requirement to stand when the Queen stands or enters a room. This rule is absolute, ensuring that everyone in the Queen's presence shows the appropriate respect.

When greeting the Queen, men are expected to bow their heads, while women curtsy. However, these curtsies are not the grand gestures often depicted in films or fairy tales; instead, they are demure and subtle, involving a slight dip down with one leg behind the other.

Public displays of affection are also frowned upon for members of the royal family, especially when traveling. This protocol is designed to avoid making those from more conservative cultures feel uncomfortable by showing signs of affection publicly.

Family Dynamics: Behind the Scenes

The royal family's dynamics are as complex as they are intriguing. The family is known for its strong sense of unity and tradition, but it is not without its challenges. For instance, the rule that heirs should not travel together to preserve the line to the throne is a significant aspect of royal life. However, Prince William and Catherine have chosen to break this tradition by traveling with their children, at least until Prince George reaches the age of 12.

The family's approach to marriage is also governed by strict protocols. According to the Royal Marriages Act of 1772, royal descendants must seek the monarch's approval before proposing. This tradition has been upheld in recent years, with the Queen approving the unions of her children and grandchildren, including Prince William's proposal to Catherine Middleton.

Unique Traditions and Customs

One of the lesser-known traditions within the royal family is the practice of always traveling with a black outfit. This protocol ensures that members of the royal family are prepared to dress in mourning attire should a death occur while they are traveling.

The Queen's use of her purse as a subtle social signal is another fascinating tradition. When she places her clutch on the table during dinner, it signals that it is time to wrap up the meal. Similarly, when she swaps her purse from her left hand to her right, it indicates that she would like to finish her conversation.

Interviews and Insights from Royal Experts

To gain deeper insights into the royal family's traditions and protocols, it is helpful to hear from those who have been close to the family. Grant Harrold, former butler to Prince Charles, offers valuable insights into the etiquette and protocol that govern royal life. According to Harrold, discussing topics such as sex, religion, politics, or money is strictly off-limits when interacting with the royals. Instead, conversations should focus on more neutral subjects like travel and the weather.

Royal biographer and historian, Andrew Morton, provides another perspective on the royal family's dynamics. Morton notes that the Queen's ability to adapt and evolve has been crucial in maintaining the monarchy's relevance. For example, her decision to allow the 2013 Succession to the Crown Act, which ensured that Princess Charlotte's place in the line of succession was secure, was a significant departure from traditional rules.

Modernizing Traditions: Queen Elizabeth II's Legacy

Queen Elizabeth II has been instrumental in modernizing certain royal traditions while maintaining others. Her decision to broadcast her coronation ceremony in 1953 marked a significant shift towards greater public engagement and transparency. This move was seen as a bold step in opening up the life of the royals to the modern world.

The Queen has also shown a willingness to break with tradition when necessary. For instance, she consented to Prince Charles's marriage to Camilla Parker Bowles, a divorcee, despite the historical prohibition on such unions. Similarly, she approved Prince Harry's marriage to Meghan Markle, another divorcee, reflecting her adaptability and understanding of changing societal norms.

Balancing Tradition and Modernity

The royal family's ability to balance tradition with modernity is a delicate but essential part of their survival. Catherine, the Duchess of Cambridge, has been a key figure in this balancing act. Her approach to royal life has been characterized by a blend of respect for tradition and a willingness to innovate. For example, her decision to show her wedding dress to the Queen during the design process was in line with royal protocol, yet her choice of a modern designer like Sarah Burton for Alexander McQueen reflected her own personal style.

Family Gatherings and Celebrations

Family gatherings are an integral part of royal life, often blending tradition with personal touches. The annual Christmas gathering at Sandringham is a prime example. This event, which involves the entire family coming together to celebrate the holiday, is steeped in tradition yet remains a deeply personal and family-oriented occasion.

The Easter Sunday service at St. George's Chapel, Windsor Castle, is another significant family tradition. Here, the royal family attends church services together, followed by a traditional lamb lunch. This event is a time for the family to come together and celebrate the religious holiday in a private yet meaningful way.

The Role of the Monarch in Modern Times

The monarch's role in modern times is multifaceted and evolving. Queen Elizabeth II has been a steadfast figure, adapting to changing times while maintaining the dignity and tradition of the monarchy. Her ability to connect with the public and her willingness to break with tradition when necessary have been key in ensuring the monarchy's continued relevance.

As Catherine prepares to take on her future role as Queen of Wales, she will face the challenge of balancing tradition with modernity. Her journey so far has shown that she is well-equipped to handle this task, combining her respect for royal protocol with her own unique approach to royal life.

The secrets and traditions of the royal family are a fascinating aspect of their lives, offering a glimpse into a world that is both familiar and mysterious. As we delve deeper into these intricacies, we gain a greater understanding of the complex dynamics that govern the British monarchy, a institution that continues to captivate and inspire people around the world.

Vision for the Future: Catherine's Aspirations and Influence

"The best way to predict the future is to create it." These words, often attributed to Abraham Lincoln, encapsulate the proactive and visionary approach that Catherine, the Princess of Wales, is taking as she prepares for her future role as queen. As the wife of Prince William, the heir apparent to the British throne, Catherine is not only learning the intricacies of royal life but also shaping her own vision for how she will influence future generations and ensure the monarchy's relevance in modern times.

Early Preparation and Learning

Catherine's journey towards becoming a future queen began long before her marriage to Prince William in 2011. After graduating from the University of St.

Andrews, she took on various roles, including working as an accessories buyer for a clothing retailer and assisting her parents' mail-order business. However, it was her engagement to Prince William that marked the beginning of her formal preparation for royal life.

Since her marriage, Catherine has been diligently learning about the roles and responsibilities of a member of the royal family. She has undertaken extensive training, including lessons in royal protocol, etiquette, and the constitutional role of the monarchy. These efforts have been complemented by her active participation in royal duties and charitable work, which have helped her gain a deeper understanding of the needs and challenges of the communities she serves.

Aspirations for Royal Life

Catherine's aspirations for her role as queen are multifaceted and reflect her commitment to both tradition and modernity. One of her primary goals is to continue the legacy of her predecessors while also bringing a fresh perspective to the monarchy. This balance is crucial in ensuring that the institution remains relevant and connected to the people it serves.

Focus on Early Childhood and Mental Health

Catherine's charitable work has been particularly focused on issues surrounding early childhood care, addiction, and mental health. In 2021, she established the Centre for Early Childhood, part of the Royal Foundation, which aims to drive positive change for young children and their families. This initiative underscores her belief in the importance of early childhood development and its impact on future generations.

Her involvement in mental health awareness is another significant aspect of her vision. Along with Prince William and Prince Harry, she launched the Heads Together initiative in 2016, which seeks to raise awareness about mental health problems and ease the stigma associated with them. This campaign has been instrumental in encouraging people to discuss their mental health openly, reflecting Catherine's commitment to creating a more compassionate and supportive society.

Influence on Future Generations

Catherine's influence on future generations will be shaped by her approach to royal duties and her engagement with the public. She has already demonstrated her ability to connect with people from all walks of life, whether through official visits, charitable work, or personal interactions.

Public Engagement and Accessibility

One of Catherine's key aspirations is to make the monarchy more accessible and relatable to the public. She has been praised for her down-to-earth approach and her willingness to engage with people in a more informal manner. This approach has helped to humanize the royal family and make it more relevant to modern society.

For instance, during the COVID-19 pandemic, Catherine and Prince William traveled extensively to pay tribute to those on the frontlines, showcasing their support and appreciation for the efforts of healthcare workers and other essential service providers. These actions not only highlighted their commitment to public service but also demonstrated their ability to adapt and respond to contemporary challenges.

Ensuring the Monarchy's Relevance

Catherine's vision for the future of the monarchy is one of continued relevance and adaptability. She understands that the institution must evolve to remain meaningful in modern times. This involves embracing new technologies, engaging with diverse communities, and addressing contemporary issues such as climate change, social inequality, and mental health.

Modernizing the Monarchy

In line with her vision, Catherine has been instrumental in modernizing certain aspects of royal life. For example, she has used social media platforms to connect with the public and share personal moments, such as family photographs and updates on her charitable work. This approach has helped to bridge the gap between the royal family and the general public, making the monarchy feel more approachable and connected to the lives of ordinary people. Additionally, Catherine has supported initiatives that promote education and awareness of various social issues. Her patronage of over 20 charitable and military organizations, including the Anna Freud Centre, Action for Children, and the National Portrait Gallery, reflects her commitment to using her platform to drive positive change.

Personal Qualities and Strengths

Catherine's personal qualities and strengths will be crucial in her future role as queen. Her ability to balance tradition with modernity, her compassion and empathy towards others, and her dedication to public service are all attributes that will serve her well.

Grace and Resilience

Throughout her journey, Catherine has demonstrated remarkable grace and resilience. Her ability to handle the intense media scrutiny and the pressures of royal life with poise and dignity has earned her widespread respect. This resilience will be essential as she faces the challenges of her new role, ensuring that she remains a steady and inspiring figure for the nation.

Family Support and Unity

Catherine's vision for the future is also deeply rooted in her family life. Her relationship with Prince William and their children—Prince George, Princess Charlotte, and Prince Louis—is a cornerstone of her strength and motivation. The family's unity and support for one another will be vital as they navigate the complexities of royal life together.

Public Perception and Expectations

The public's perception of Catherine has been overwhelmingly positive, reflecting her hard work and genuine commitment to her role. As she prepares to become queen, there is a sense of anticipation and expectation about how she will shape the monarchy's future.

A New Era for the Monarchy

Catherine's ascension to the role of queen will mark a new era for the British monarchy. Her vision, aspirations, and influence will be instrumental in shaping the institution's relevance and impact in modern times. As she continues to learn, grow, and adapt, she will undoubtedly become a powerful force in ensuring the monarchy's continued significance and connection to the people it serves.

In the words of a royal household source, *"She is an adoring mother, and she is contributing publicly in the way we would want her to. You see it more and more. The young student has turned into our future Queen."* This sentiment captures the essence of Catherine's journey and her readiness to take on the responsibilities and challenges of her future role.

As Catherine looks to the future, her dedication to her family, her charitable work, and her commitment to the monarchy's relevance will be the guiding principles that shape her vision and influence. Her story is one of grace, strength, and a deep-seated desire to make a positive impact on the world around her.

Conclusion

"To be a princess is to play at life. To be a queen is to be a serious player...The purpose of life as a woman is to ascend to the throne and rule with heart." - Oprah Winfrey

As we draw the curtains on this exploration of Catherine's life, we find ourselves at the threshold of a new era for the British monarchy. Catherine, the Princess of Wales, stands poised to become the next Queen Consort, a role that will undoubtedly draw upon every facet of her character, every lesson learned, and every challenge overcome. In this conclusion, we will delve into the key themes that have defined Catherine's journey thus far - grace, secrets, and strength - and contemplate the legacy she may leave as a future queen.

Grace: The Hallmark of a Future Queen

Grace has been a defining characteristic of Catherine's public persona since her first steps into the royal limelight. This grace manifests in multiple ways:

1. Poise Under Pressure

From the earliest days of her relationship with Prince William, Catherine has faced intense media scrutiny. Yet, she has consistently maintained a calm and collected demeanor, rarely if ever allowing the pressure to visibly affect her. This composure under fire has earned her respect from both the public and the media.

During moments of intense public interest, such as her wedding day or the births of her children, Catherine has displayed remarkable poise. Her ability to smile for the cameras mere hours after giving birth, looking immaculate despite having just undergone labor, speaks volumes about her self-control and understanding of her public role.

2. Diplomatic Finesse

Catherine's grace extends to her interactions on the global stage. During royal tours and state visits, she has shown a natural aptitude for diplomacy. Whether it's respectfully participating in local customs, wearing clothes that pay homage to host nations, or engaging warmly with people from all walks of life, Catherine has proven herself to be a valuable asset to British soft power.

Her ability to strike the right tone in diverse situations - from formal state dinners to casual engagements with children - demonstrates a nuanced understanding of her role as a representative of the Crown. This diplomatic grace will be invaluable as she takes on more senior responsibilities in the future.

3. Graceful Evolution

Perhaps one of the most remarkable aspects of Catherine's grace has been her ability to evolve into her royal role without losing her authentic self. She has gracefully transitioned from a commoner to a duchess, and now to the Princess of Wales, adapting to each new level of responsibility with apparent ease.

This evolution has been evident in her style, her public speaking, and her choice of patronages. Catherine has grown into her role organically, taking on more significant responsibilities as she's become more established within the royal family. Her grace in this evolution serves as a model for how modern royalty can adapt to changing times while maintaining the dignity of their position.

4. Grace in Personal Relationships

While much of Catherine's life is lived in the public eye, glimpses of her personal relationships reveal a grace that extends beyond her public persona. Her closeness with her own family, her apparent warm relationship with her in-laws, and her dedication to her children all speak to a graceful approach to personal relationships.

This grace in her personal life lends authenticity to her public role, particularly in her work with family-oriented charities and her advocacy for early childhood development. It allows her to connect genuinely with the public on issues related to family and child-rearing.

Secrets: The Power of Privacy in a Public Life

The theme of secrets in Catherine's life is not about scandalous revelations, but rather about the power of maintaining privacy and discretion in a role that demands so much public exposure. This aspect of Catherine's approach to royal life has several dimensions:

1. Guarding Family Privacy

Despite intense public interest, Catherine has been remarkably successful in maintaining a level of privacy for her family, particularly her children. She and William have been deliberate in controlling the public's access to their children, releasing photographs on their own terms and limiting public appearances.

This protective approach extends to Catherine's own family. While the

Middletons have inevitably been thrust into the spotlight due to their connection to the royal family, Catherine has largely managed to shield them from undue public scrutiny. This ability to maintain boundaries between public and private life will be crucial as she moves closer to the throne.

2. The Power of Discretion

Throughout her time in the royal family, Catherine has demonstrated a high level of discretion. She rarely, if ever, speaks out of turn or reveals information that isn't carefully considered. This discretion has earned her the trust of the royal family and the respect of the public.

In an era where oversharing is common, Catherine's ability to maintain an air of mystery while still seeming relatable is a remarkable feat. It adds to her regal bearing and reinforces the special nature of the monarchy.

3. Strategic Revelation

While Catherine is generally private, she has shown a strategic approach to revealing personal information when it aligns with her charitable work. For instance, she has spoken about her own experiences with motherhood when promoting initiatives related to early childhood development. These carefully chosen moments of openness serve to humanize her and add weight to her advocacy work.

4. The Secret of Normalcy

Perhaps one of the best-kept secrets of Catherine's life is the degree of normalcy she has managed to maintain despite her extraordinary circumstances. Reports suggest that behind palace doors, the Waleses strive for as normal a family life as possible. This secret commitment to normalcy may well be a key factor in

Catherine's ability to remain grounded and relatable despite her elevated status.

Strength: The Foundation of a Future Queen

The theme of strength runs like a golden thread through Catherine's story, manifesting in various forms:

1. Mental Resilience

From the early days of her relationship with William, when she was dubbed *"Waity Katie"* by the press, to navigating the complexities of royal life, Catherine has displayed remarkable mental resilience. She has weathered media storms, family crises, and the pressures of public scrutiny with a strength that belies her gentle exterior.

This mental fortitude will be invaluable as she takes on the weighty responsibilities of queenship. The ability to remain steady in the face of challenges is a crucial quality for a monarch's consort.

2. Strength in Purpose

Catherine's strength is evident in her commitment to her chosen causes. Her work in early childhood development, for instance, demonstrates a willingness to tackle complex, long-term issues rather than opting for more immediately gratifying charitable work. This strength of purpose suggests a deep understanding of the potential impact of her royal platform.

As she's grown into her royal role, Catherine has shown increasing confidence in advocating for her causes. Her ability to speak passionately and knowledgeably about her areas of focus indicates a strength of conviction that will serve her well as queen.

3. Physical Strength and Wellness

Catherine's commitment to physical fitness and overall wellness is well-documented. From her love of sports to her apparent ease with outdoor activities during royal engagements, she presents an image of physical vitality. This emphasis on physical strength and health sets a positive example and contributes to her image as a modern, active royal.

4. Strength in Relationships

The strength of Catherine's relationships - with her husband, her children, her family of origin, and the royal family - is a key element of her success in royal life. Her apparently solid marriage to William, in particular, provides a strong foundation for their future roles as king and queen.

This relational strength extends to her public role as well. Catherine has shown an ability to form meaningful connections with people from all walks of life, a crucial skill for a future queen.

5. Adaptive Strength

One of Catherine's most important strengths is her adaptability. She has shown a remarkable ability to adjust to the demands of royal life, growing into her role with apparent ease. This adaptive strength will be crucial as she continues to take on more senior roles within the royal family.

6. Strength in Authenticity

Perhaps one of Catherine's greatest strengths is her ability to remain authentically herself despite the pressures of her role. She has managed to adapt to royal life without losing her core identity, a balancing act that requires significant inner strength.

Reflecting on Catherine's Potential Legacy as a Future Queen

As we look towards Catherine's future as Queen Consort, several potential aspects of her legacy come into focus:

1. Modernizing the Monarchy

Catherine, along with William, represents a new generation of royalty. Her background as a commoner, her education, and her approach to royal duties all contribute to a more modern image of the monarchy. As queen, she may play a significant role in continuing to modernize the institution while maintaining its traditions and dignity.

2. Advocacy for Early Childhood Development

Catherine's work in early childhood development has the potential to be a defining aspect of her legacy. Her long-term commitment to this cause, coupled with her ability to bring attention and resources to the issue, could result in significant positive changes in this field. As queen, she would have an even larger platform to advance this work.

3. Mental Health Awareness

Together with William and Harry, Catherine has been a strong advocate for mental health awareness. This work has already made a significant impact, and as queen, she could continue to reduce stigma and promote understanding around mental health issues.

4. Style and Fashion Influence

While perhaps less weighty than her charitable work, Catherine's influence on fashion and style is likely to be a notable part of her legacy. Her ability to blend high street with high-end fashion, her support of

British designers, and her elegant, appropriate style have already made her a fashion icon. As queen, her fashion choices will continue to be influential and could be used strategically to support British fashion and industry.

5. Family-Centered Monarchy

Catherine's emphasis on family, both in her personal life and in her charitable work, may contribute to a legacy of a more family-centered monarchy. This focus could help to keep the royal family relatable and in touch with the experiences of ordinary citizens.

6. Diplomatic Soft Power

Catherine's natural diplomacy and her ability to charm on the global stage suggest that as queen, she could be a significant asset to British soft power. Her legacy might include strengthened international relationships and a positive global image for Britain.

7. Stability and Continuity

In an era of rapid change and uncertainty, Catherine's steady presence and gradual, graceful evolution into her royal role may contribute to a legacy of stability. As queen, she could represent continuity and reliability, important qualities for a hereditary monarchy.

8. Redefining Queenship

As a thoroughly modern woman who will become queen, Catherine has the opportunity to redefine what queenship means in the 21st century. Her legacy might include a new model of an active, engaged Queen Consort who balances tradition with contemporary relevance.

9. Environmental Advocacy

Both Catherine and William have shown a strong commitment to environmental causes. As queen, Catherine could use her platform to advance significant environmental initiatives, potentially leaving a lasting impact on conservation efforts and climate change mitigation.

10. A Model of Grace Under Pressure

Perhaps one of Catherine's most enduring legacies will be her example of maintaining grace, dignity, and authenticity in the face of intense public scrutiny. Her ability to navigate the challenges of royal life while remaining true to herself could serve as an inspiration not just to future royals, but to people in all walks of life.

Challenges and Opportunities Ahead

As Catherine looks towards her future role as Queen Consort, she faces both challenges and opportunities:

1. Evolving Monarchy

The role of the monarchy in contemporary society is continually evolving. Catherine, along with William, will need to navigate how to keep the institution relevant and valuable in changing times. This may involve carefully balancing tradition with modernization.

2. Global Challenges

As the future queen, Catherine will need to engage with complex global issues such as climate change, economic inequality, and international conflicts. Her ability to understand and thoughtfully address these challenges will be crucial.

3. Media Scrutiny

While Catherine has handled media attention admirably so far, the scrutiny is likely to intensify as she moves closer to becoming queen. Continuing to manage this pressure while maintaining her privacy and authenticity will be an ongoing challenge.

4. Expanding Influence

As Queen Consort, Catherine will have an expanded platform to influence policy and public opinion. Learning to wield this influence effectively and responsibly will be a key challenge and opportunity.

5. Balancing Roles

Catherine will need to balance her roles as wife, mother, public figure, and queen. Finding harmony among these different aspects of her life will be crucial for her personal wellbeing and public success.

The Road Ahead

As Catherine continues her journey towards becoming Queen Consort, she carries with her the lessons, experiences, and qualities that have defined her life thus far. Her grace in the face of pressure, her ability to keep certain aspects of her life private, and her inner strength have all contributed to her success as the Princess of Wales. These same qualities will undoubtedly serve her well as she steps into the role of queen.

Catherine's potential to leave a lasting, positive impact on the monarchy and on British society is significant. Her dedication to important causes, her ability to connect with people from all walks of life, and her model of graceful, strong womanhood position her to be not just a consort, but a true partner to the future king and a beloved figure in her own right.

As she faces the challenges and opportunities that lie ahead, Catherine's journey will continue to captivate and inspire. Her story is far from over; indeed, in many ways, it feels as though it's just beginning. The grace, secrets, and strength that have characterized her life so far will undoubtedly continue to shape her path as she moves towards her destiny as the future Queen of Wales.

In Catherine, we see the potential for a queen who embodies the best of tradition and modernity, and who can relate to the everyday experiences of her people while also representing the dignity and continuity of the crown. Her journey from commoner to future queen is a testament to her character, a reflection of a changing monarchy, and a source of fascination for people around the world.

As we conclude this biography, we look forward with great anticipation to the next chapters of Catherine's story. The grace she has shown, the secrets she has kept, and the strength she has demonstrated have laid a solid foundation for her future role. How she will build upon this foundation as Queen Consort remains to be seen, but if her past is any indication, Catherine is more than equal to the task that awaits her.

In Catherine, the future Queen of Wales, we see a woman poised to make her mark on history - not through grand gestures or radical changes, but through the steady, graceful execution of her duties, the thoughtful application of her influence, and the strength of her character. As she steps ever closer to the throne, Catherine carries with her the hopes, admiration, and good wishes of millions around the world, all eager to see how her remarkable story will unfold.